A Century of Stories

New Hanover County Public Library

1906-2006

Rookie Read-About™ Science

The Sun Is Always Shining Somewhere

By Allan Fowler

Images supplied by VALAN Photos

Consultants:
Robert L. Hillerich, Ph.D., Bowling Green
State University, Bowling Green, Ohio

Mary Nalbandian, Director of Science,
Chicago Public Schools, Chicago, Illinois

Fay Robinson, Child Development Specialist

CHILDRENS PRESS ®
CHICAGO

Series cover and interior design by Sara Shelton

Library of Congress Cataloging-in-Publication Data

Fowler, Allan.
    The sun is always shining somewhere / by Allan Fowler.
      p.   cm.—(Rookie read-about science)
    Summary: Examines the sun in the context of other, more distant stars
and discusses the night sky and movement of the earth.
    ISBN 0-516-04906-2
    1. Sun—Juvenile literature. 2. Astronomy—Juvenile literature. [1. Sun.
2. Astronomy.] I. Title. II. Series.
    QB521.5.F69 1990
    523.7—dc20
                                                    90-2176
                                                  CIP
                                                  AC

The sun is very important
to us.

You and I need the sun to
grow and be healthy.

Plants need the sun to grow

and blossom.

Animals need sunshine, too.

Sunshine makes many good things happen.

Tomatoes ripen

and so do pumpkins.

Did you know that the sun
is a star?

It looks bigger than other stars. But it's not.

The sun looks bigger than other stars because it's closer to us than other stars.

Here's one way you can think about why the sun looks bigger than other stars in the sky.

An airplane flying high in the sky looks very small, doesn't it?

But if you've been to the airport and seen an airplane up close, you know that it is really very big.

In the same way, the sun looks bigger than other, faraway stars.

The sun never stops shining.

Do you know why you can't see the sun at night?

To find the answer, turn on a lamp in a dark room.

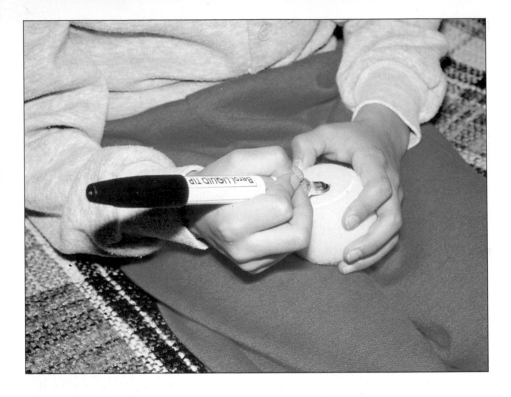

Put a tiny mark on a ball.
Pretend the mark is you.
Imagine the ball is the
Earth.

Now hold the ball in front
of the lamp. Slowly turn
the ball around.

The part of it that was
lit up by the lamp before
is now in the dark.

The part that was dark
before is now in the light.

Earth is like a ball—
a very big ball.

It is always turning.

It turns out of the sunlight
and into the dark of night.

then back into the sunlight
the next morning.

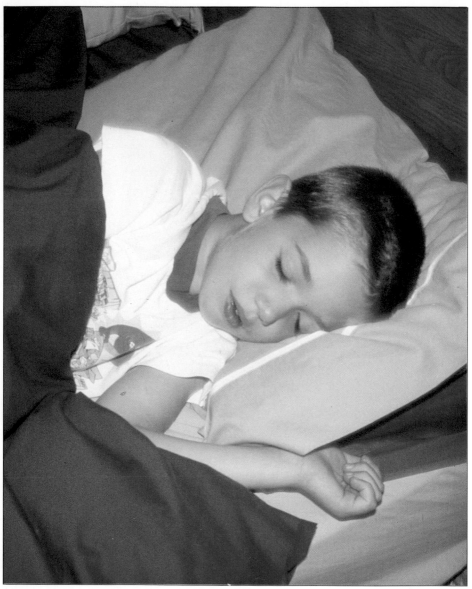

Isn't this nice to know?

Even when you're asleep at night, the sun is always shining—somewhere.

Words You Know

sun

warmth

sunlight

star

Earth

night

morning

Index

About the Author

Allan Fowler is a free-lance writer with a background in advertising. Born in New York, he lives in Chicago now and enjoys traveling.

Photo Credits

Valan—© Irwin Barrett, Cover; © John Cancalosi, 3; © Phil Norton, 5, 9, 31 (bottom right); © Kennon Cooke, 6, 18, 30 (top right); © John Fowler, 7; © Eastcott-Momatiuk, 8; © Val Whelan, 11, 12; © Stephen J. Krasemann, 17; © J. A. Wilkinson, 21, 23, 24; © V. Wilkinson, 22, 28; © Wayne Lankinen, 30 (top left); © Gerhard Kahrmann, 30 (bottom); © Brian Atkinson, 31 (bottom left)

Hansen Planetarium—14, 31 (top left)

NASA—26, 27, 31 (top right)

COVER: Sunrise and small boats

ML

2/OC